King Thrushbeard

Retold by
Kelly Morrow

Printed with support from the Waldorf Curriculum Fund

Published by:
Waldorf Publications at the
Research Institute for Waldorf Education
38 Main Street
Chatham, NY 12037

Title: *King Thrushbeard*
Author and Illustrator: Kelly Morrow
Editor: David Mitchell
Proofreader: Ann Erwin
Cover: David Mitchell
Cover Art: Kelly Morrow
© 2010 by AWSNA
ISBN #978-1-936367-04-7
Printed by McNaughton & Gunn
Saline, MI 48176 USA
June 2010

Second printing 2014
CreateSpace On-Demand Publishing

Chapter I

Once upon a time, a king had a daughter. She was quite beautiful, but proud and haughty. No suitor was good enough for her. She sent away one after the other. She ridiculed them as well.

Once the king planned a great feast. He invited from far and near all young men who were likely to marry. They were lined up according to their rank and standing.

First came the kings, then the grand dukes. Then came the princes and earls.

The king's daughter was led down the line. To each one, she had some objection to make. One was too fat, "As big as a barrel," she said.

Another was too tall, "Long and thin has little in." The third was too short, "Short and thick is never quick." The fourth was too pale, "As pale as a ghost."

The fifth was too red, "Like a rooster!" The sixth was not straight enough, "Like a crooked branch from a tree."

So, she had something to say against each one. She made the most fun of a good king who stood near the front of the line. His chin had grown a little crooked.

"Look," she cried and laughed. "He has a chin like a thrush's beak!"

From that time on he was called King Thrushbeard.

When the old king saw that his daughter did nothing but mock the young men, he was very angry. He promised that she would have the very first beggar who came to his doors as her husband.

Chapter II

A few days later, a fiddler came and sang beneath the window, trying to earn a few pennies. When the king heard him, he said, "Let him come up." So, the fiddler came in with his dirty, ragged clothes. He sang before the king and his daughter. When he had ended, he asked for a token gift. The king said, "Your song has pleased me so well that I will give you my daughter to be your wife." The king's daughter shuddered.

But the king said, I have promised to give you to the very first beggar who came. I will keep that promise." All she could say mattered not.

The priest was brought. She had to be married to the fiddler. When that was done, the king said, "Now it is not proper for you, a beggar woman, to stay any longer in my palace. You must go away with your husband." The beggar led her out by her hand. She had to walk away on foot with him.

When they came to a large forest, she asked, "To whom does that lovely forest belong?"

"It belongs to King Thrushbeard. If you had chosen him as your husband, it would be yours now."

"Ah, what an unhappy woman I am. If I had only married King Thrushbeard!"

Then, they came to a meadow. She asked, "To whom

does this beautiful green meadow belong?"

"It belongs to King Thrushbeard. If you had chosen him as your husband, it would be yours now."

"Ah, what an unhappy woman I am. If I had only married King Thrushbeard!"

Then, they came to a large town. She asked again, "To whom does this fine large town belong?"

"It belongs to King Thrushbeard. If you had chosen him as your husband, it would be yours now."

"Ah, what an unhappy woman I am. If I had only married King Thrushbeard!"

"It does not please me," said the beggar, "to hear you always wishing for another husband. Am I not good enough for you?"

Chapter III

At last, they came to a very little hut, and she said, "Oh goodness! What a small house! To whom does this miserable, tiny hut belong?"

The beggar answered, "This is my house and yours, where we shall live together."

She had to bend down to go in the door. "Where are the servants?" asked the king's daughter.

"What servants?" answered the beggar.

"You must do whatever you wish to have done. Make a fire at once. We must cook our dinner. I am quite hungry."

But the king's daughter knew nothing about lighting fires or cooking. The beggar had to show her to get it started at all. When they had finished their small meal, they went to bed.

For a few days, they lived this way as well as they could. Then, they had no food left in the house. "Wife, we cannot go on any longer eating and drinking like this and earning nothing. You must make baskets to sell for money."

Then, she began to make baskets. The tough willows hurt her delicate hands.

"I see that this will not do," said the man.

"You had better spin. Perhaps you can do that better." She sat down and tried to spin. The hard thread cut
her soft fingers so that they bled.

"See," said the man, "you are fit for no sort of work. I have made a bad bargain with you. Now I will make a business of earthen pots. You must sit in the marketplace and sell them."

"Oh, no," she thought.

"If any of the people from my father's kingdom come to the market and see me sitting there, selling, how they will make fun of me." But it was of no use. She had to do this or choose to die of hunger.

Chapter IV

For the first time, she did well. For the people were glad to buy the woman's pots as she was quite beautiful.

They paid her what she asked. Many even gave her the money and left without the pots.

So, they lived on what she had earned as long as it lasted.

Then the husband bought some new earthen pots. His wife sat down at the corner of the marketplace and set out the pots, ready for sale.

But, suddenly, there came a drunken rider on a horse galloping along. He rode right through the earthenware pots so that they were all broken into a thousand bits.

She began to weep and did not know what to do. "Alas! What will happen to me?" she cried. "What will my husband say to this?"

She ran home and told him of this misfortune. "Who would seat herself at a corner of the marketplace with earthenware pots?" asked the man. "Stop the crying. I see very well that you cannot do any ordinary work. So, I went to the king's palace and have asked whether they had a job for a kitchen maid. They have promised me that they will take you. In that way, you will get your food for nothing."

Chapter V

The king's daughter was now a kitchen maid and had to do whatever the cook said. She had to do the dirtiest work of all. In each of her pockets she fastened a little jar, in which she took home her share of the left-over scraps. This is what they ate for food.

It happened that the wedding of the king's eldest son was to be celebrated. The poor woman went up and placed herself by the door of the hall to watch. When all the candles were lit, people, each more beautiful than the other, entered. All was full of splendor. She thought of where she was now with a sad heart. She cursed the pride and haughtiness which had humbled her and brought her to poverty.

The smell of the delicious dishes which were being taken in and out reached her.

Now and then, the servants threw her a few morsels of them. These she put in her jars to take home.

All at once, the king's son entered, clothed in velvet and silk with gold chains. When he saw the beautiful kitchen maid standing by the door, he took her by the hand. He would have danced with her, but she refused and shrank from fear. She saw it was King Thrushbeard, her suitor whom she had driven away with scorn.

He did not turn away. He drew her into the hall, but the jars in her pockets moved about and fell to the ground and broke. The food was scattered everywhere. When the people saw this, there arose laughter, and she was so ashamed that she would rather have been thousands of feet below the ground.

She ran to the door and would have run away, but on the stairs a man caught her and brought her back. When she looked at him, it was King Thrushbeard again.

He said to her kindly, "Do not be afraid. I am the beggar who has been living with you in that wretched hut. For love of you, I disguised myself so. I also was the rider on the horse who rode through your pots. This was all done to humble your haughty ways, and to punish you for mocking me."

Then she wept bitterly and said, "I have done great wrong. I am not worthy to be your wife."

But he said, "Be comforted. Those days have passed. Now we will celebrate our true wedding." Then the maids-in-waiting came and put on her the most splendid clothing. Her father and his whole court came and wished happiness in her marriage to King Thrushbeard. Then, the joy began in earnest.

Made in the USA
Monee, IL
27 June 2020

King Thrushbeard

A haughty princess cannot believe that she must marry a beggar. She certainly cannot live such a lowly life!

Waldorf
PUBLICATIONS

38 Main Street
Chatham, NY 12037

ISBN 978-1-936367-04-7